MEASURING

Science
Experiences

FRANKLIN WATTS, INC.
845 Third Avenue • New York, N.Y. 10022

MEASURING

written and illustrated by

Jeanne Bendick

OCLC#196474
SBN 531-01435-5
Library of Congress Catalog Card Number: 76-150734

MEASURING

Suppose you have a box that looks like this.

And you want to tell a lot of people, who have never seen it, exactly what the box is like. How many things can you tell them about the box?

Can you tell them how big it is?

How can you do that?

6

Can you tell them how much it holds?
How can you do that?
Can you tell them how much the box weighs?
How can you do that?

7

You can measure those things.
You can measure how tall the box is.
You can measure how long and how wide it is.
You can measure how much it holds.
You can measure how heavy it is.
If you measure all those things, you can tell a lot about the box.

What does "measuring" mean?

What do you do when you measure something?

First, you ask yourself a question — maybe, "How high is the box?" or "How much can I put in it?"

Then you find the answer by comparing the box with something else.

But what do you compare the box with?

That depends on what you want to know.

THINK FOR YOURSELF

Could you use the same way of measuring to find out
how tall the box is,
how much it holds,
and how heavy it is?

If you are not sure, turn the page.

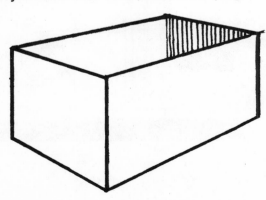

There are different ways of measuring.

You use one way of measuring to find out how long and how wide and how tall something is. You could compare it with a ruler or a stick to find out those things.

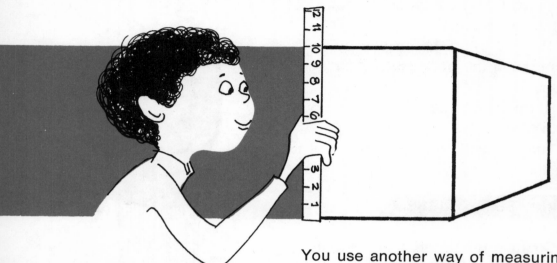

You use another way of measuring to find out how heavy something is. Maybe you could compare it with a pound of butter or a half-pound candy bar.

If you want to find out how much a bowl holds, you could compare it with how much a cup or a carton holds.

Each time, you compare the thing you want to measure with some measurement you have.

Measuring is comparing.

Whatever you are comparing against is your *unit of measure.*

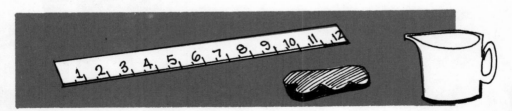

How tall are you?

You can compare yourself with a ruler. The ruler is your unit of measure.

Maybe you are as tall as five 1-foot rulers.

You can compare yourself with your sister. Then your sister is the unit of measure.

Maybe you are twice as tall as your sister.

You can compare yourself with the height of the room. When you do that, the room is your unit of measure.

Maybe you are half as tall as the room.

You can use any unit of measure you want.

But when you tell how tall you are, you have to tell what unit you used.

You can say that you are 2 sisters tall or 1/2 room tall — or even 45 paper clips tall, if you want to.

14

People who can see the unit of measure you used will know just how you compare to it and how tall you are.

But suppose they cannot see your unit? Sisters come in different sizes. So do rooms and paper clips.

SISTERS

THINK FOR YOURSELF

How could you communicate your unit of measure to someone in another place?

15

You could cut a piece of string the height of your sister and send the string.

You could mark on a big piece of paper how tall your sister is and mail the paper.

You could cut a stick that long and send the stick.

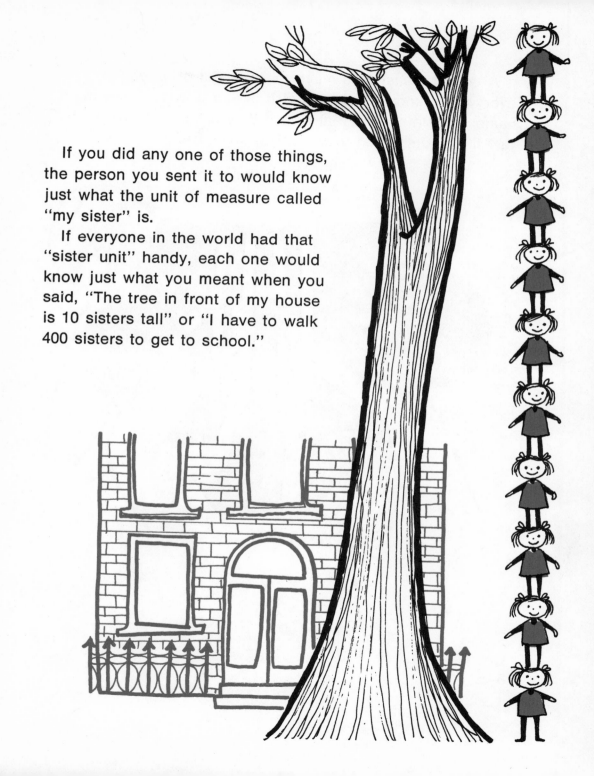

If you did any one of those things, the person you sent it to would know just what the unit of measure called "my sister" is.

If everyone in the world had that "sister unit" handy, each one would know just what you meant when you said, "The tree in front of my house is 10 sisters tall" or "I have to walk 400 sisters to get to school."

A unit of measure is much more useful if people everywhere know exactly what it is and if it is always the same. People can do that only if they have their own units, just like yours, when they want to compare.

18

People have agreed on many kinds of measuring units. If you say that you are 5 feet tall, someone halfway around the world, who does not even speak the same language, can find out exactly how tall you are.

That is because a foot is a *standard* unit of measure. A standard unit of measure is the same everywhere and it does not change.

THINK FOR YOURSELF

How do you think people first invented units of measure?

How do you think the unit "a foot" began?

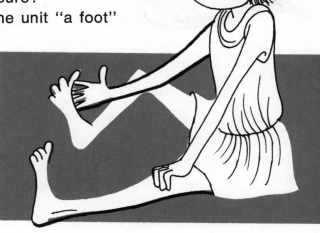

19

Take a ruler or a tape measure.

Borrow your father or your big brother or an uncle.

Measure his foot and write down how long it is.

Start a list and write each measurement down.

Measure how wide his thumb is.

Have him take a step, and measure how long the step is.

Have him stretch out his arm. Measure from his nose to the end of his fingers.

Have him stretch out both arms, holding a string. Then measure the length of the string from one hand to the other.

When you have finished, turn the page.

20

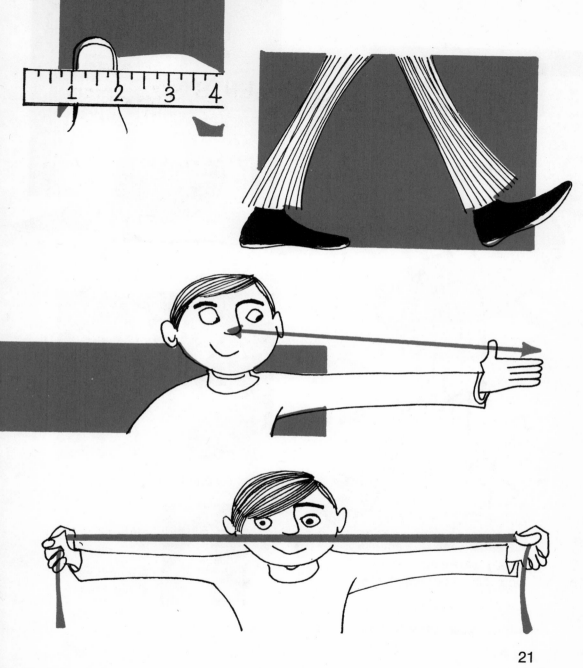

HOW SOME MEASUREMENTS STARTED

A Roman pace was about 5 feet.
1,000 paces made a mile.
How long is our mile today?

For the answers to questions, see page 70.

A foot was anywhere
from 11 to 14 inches.

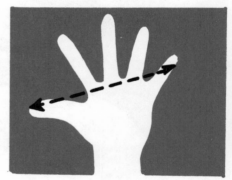

A span was 9 inches.

A thumb was
about 1 inch.

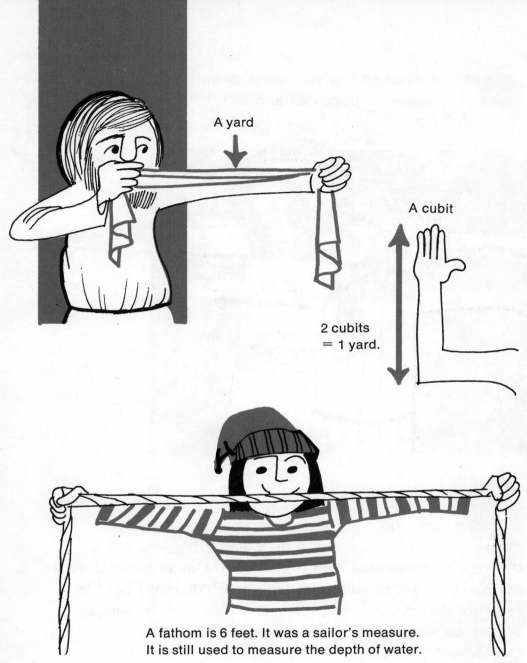

A yard

A cubit

2 cubits
= 1 yard.

A fathom is 6 feet. It was a sailor's measure.
It is still used to measure the depth of water.

Are the measurements you wrote down anything like the units of measure on pages 22 and 23?

A long time ago, people used the handiest units of measure — themselves. But a man with a big foot got a different measurement than a man with a small foot did. And the reach of a man with long arms was different from the reach of a man with short arms. So, after a while, people agreed on standard units that would be the same everywhere.

24

Can you use yourself to figure out some other units of measure? Or to invent new units?

MEASURING "HOW LONG"

When we want to measure how long something is, we measure the distance from the beginning to the end of it, along a line. This is called *linear* (LIN-ee-uhr) measure.

You can use linear measure to measure in any direction. If you are measuring a box, you use linear measure to see how long it is, and how wide, and how high.

You can measure any object with linear measure.

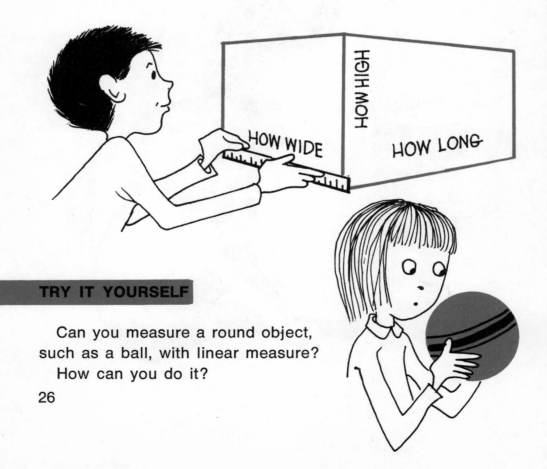

TRY IT YOURSELF

Can you measure a round object, such as a ball, with linear measure?
How can you do it?

26

You can measure any distance, as long as you have a place to start and a place to stop.

You can measure the distance from one end of a pencil to the other,

or the distance from your house to school,

or the distance from the earth to the moon, if you know how.

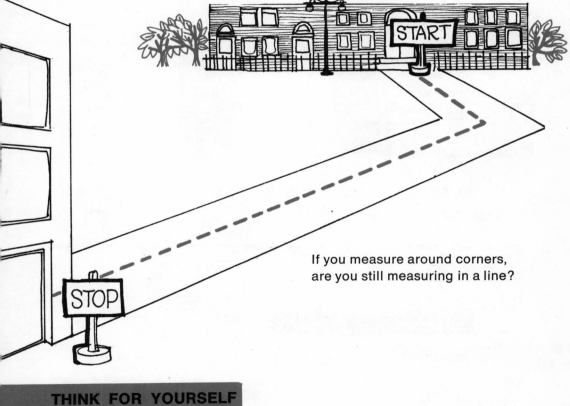

If you measure around corners, are you still measuring in a line?

THINK FOR YOURSELF

What does "how far" mean?

When you measure distance along a line, you can use the same unit of measure over and over again, end to end, from the place where you start to the place where you stop. You count the number of times you used that unit.

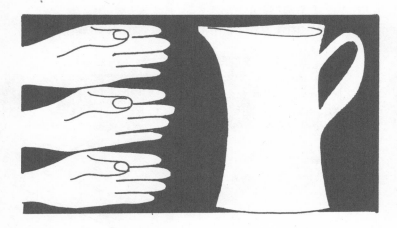

The pitcher is 3 hands high.

You can also use a scale, such as a foot ruler, where the counting is already done for you.

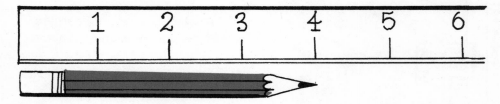

For some things, you may use a unit once or only a few times.

The pencil is 4 inches long.

Sometimes you use the unit many times. The distance around Earth at the equator is 24,902 miles.

What would happen if you used two or three different units to measure one length?

Measure the top of a table, using a foot ruler.

Tell how long the table is.

Measure it again, using the ruler, a pencil, and your shoe, in turn.

Tell how long the table is in ruler-pencil-shoe measurement.

About 5 feet tall

The units of length you probably use most are the inch, the foot, and the yard.

12 inches = 1 foot.

3 feet, or 36 inches = 1 yard.

These standard units of length are used in some English-speaking countries. They are part of the English, or Imperial, system of measuring. But that does not mean that they are used by most of the people in the world.

Most people use a system of measuring called the metric system.

More people in the world would understand how tall you were if, instead of saying that you were about 5 feet tall, you said that you were about 1-1/2 meters tall. Or about 1 meter, 5 decimeters tall.

That sounds more complicated than feet or inches. Why do so many people use the metric system?

About 1-1/2 meters tall

Take two stiff strips of cardboard and make two small rulers. Make one like this, marked off in inches.

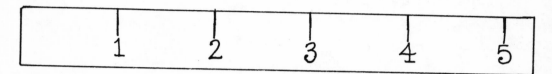

The distance between each mark is 1 inch.
Make the other like this.

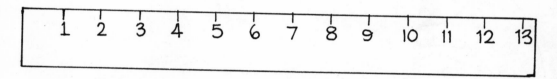

Put the marks exactly where they are in the picture. The distance between each mark is 1 centimeter.

This is a metric ruler.

When you are measuring big things with your inch ruler, you have to remember that 12 inches make a foot, which is the next larger unit of measure in the English system. If you are measuring very big things you have to remember that 36 inches, or 3 feet, make a yard, which is the unit next larger than a foot.

If you want to measure something quite small — say 1/2 inch — what part of a foot is that? What part of a yard is that? See if you can figure it out.

Now look at your metric ruler, marked off in centimeters. Ten centimeters make a decimeter, which is the next larger unit. One decimeter is 10 times longer than a centimeter.

The next larger unit is the meter. A meter is 10 times longer than a decimeter.

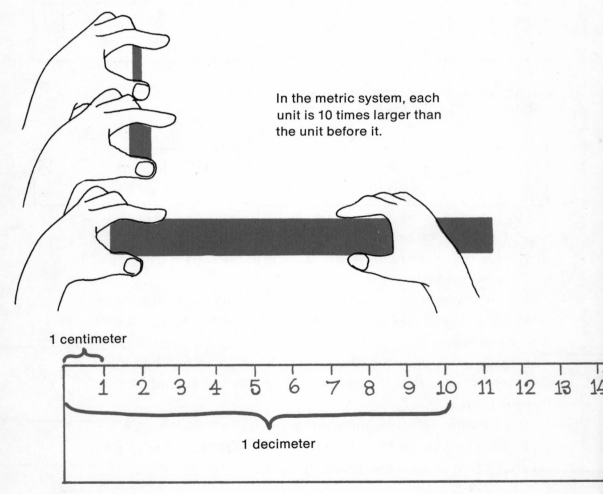

In the metric system, each unit is 10 times larger than the unit before it.

1 centimeter

1 2 3 4 5 6 7 8 9 10 11 12 13 14

1 decimeter

All measurements of length in the metric system are based on the meter. A decimeter is 1/10 of a meter. *Deci* means "one-tenth."

A centimeter is 1/100 of a meter. What do you think *centi* means?

If you want to measure something very small — say 1/10 centimeter — you have a unit for that, too. It is called a millimeter.

Can you make some millimeter marks on your metric ruler? Can you figure out how many millimeters there are in a meter? What do you think *milli* means?

TRY IT YOURSELF

Find a long strip of cardboard, or fasten two strips together, and make a meterstick.

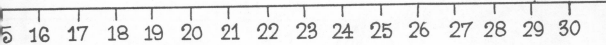

5 16 17 18 19 20 21 22 23 24 25 26 27 28 29 30

How many numerals would you have to write before you measured 1 meter? ⟶

Now use both rulers to measure some of the things around you. (Measure to the nearest whole number.)

Measure this book, from top to bottom.

Measure a pencil.

Measure your foot.

Measure a paper clip.

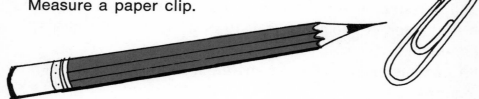

Measure how wide a door is. Measure the distance from one end of the room to the other. Measure a lot of things — big things and little things.

Write down the measurements in inches and in centimeters.

	inches	approximate centimeters
pencil	4	10
foot	8	21
room	118	300

Now do some arithmetic with your measurements.

First, where you have made big measurements in inches, change the inches into feet or yards.

Where you have small measurements, change the inches into smaller units. Can you do that?

Now, where you have made big measurements in centimeters, change the centimeters into decimeters or meters.

Where you have small measurements, change the centimeters to millimeters.

Which measurements are easier to work with?
Why is that?

The metric system is a decimal system. (Do you remember what *deci* means?)

Can you think of something that we use a decimal system for? What are you saying when you say that something costs 4 dollars and 28 cents?

You are saying that it costs
4 dollars (which are hundreds),
2 dimes (which are tens),
and 8 cents (which are ones).
Or you can say that it costs 428 cents.

4   2   8   100 100 100 100 28

Is that anything like saying that the room is 4 meters, 2 decimeters, and 8 centimeters long?

In the English system,
12 inches   = 1 foot,
3 feet   = 1 yard,
5-1/2 yards   = 1 rod,
5,280 feet   = 1 mile.

In the metric system,
10 millimeters   = 1 centimeter,
10 centimeters   = 1 decimeter,
10 decimeters   = 1 meter,
10 meters   = 1 decameter,
10 decameters   = 1 hectometer,
10 hectometers   = 1 kilometer,
(or 1,000 meters).

1 kilometer   = .621 mile (or
               about 5/8 of a mile),

1 centimeter = .3937 inch,
1 meter   = 39.37 inches.

37

CHOOSING YOUR UNIT

Measuring is easier if you choose the right unit of measure. It would take a long time to measure from the front of the house to the back, 1 inch or 1 centimeter at a time. You can measure faster with a yardstick or a meterstick.

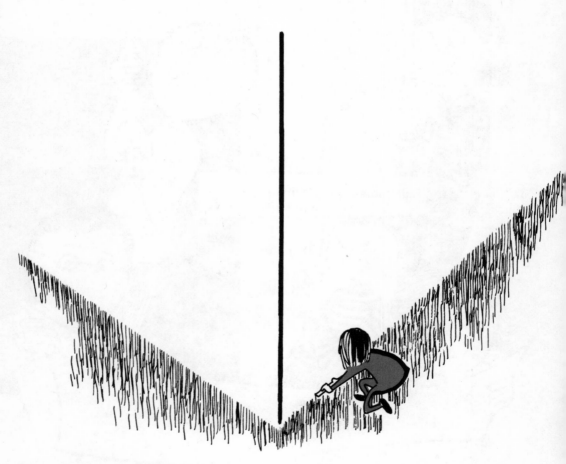

But you would have a hard time using a yardstick or a meterstick to measure a ladybug.

When you are measuring big things, a big unit is handier.

When you are measuring small things, you can measure more accurately with a small unit.

Sometimes a measurement is in between.

You can say that this flower is between 3 and 4 inches high. Or you can say that it is between 8 and 9 centimeters high.

TRY IT YOURSELF

Use your inch ruler and your centimeter ruler to see which measurement is more accurate.

Now make another inch ruler. Mark it like this, into 1/16 inches.

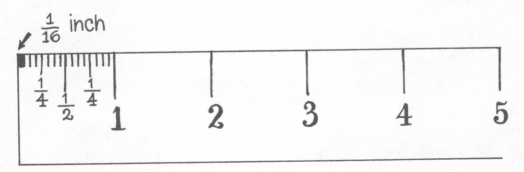

$\frac{1}{16}$ inch

How many 1/16-inch divisions are in 1 inch?
How many millimeter divisions are in 1 centimeter?
Which is easier to do arithmetic with?

40

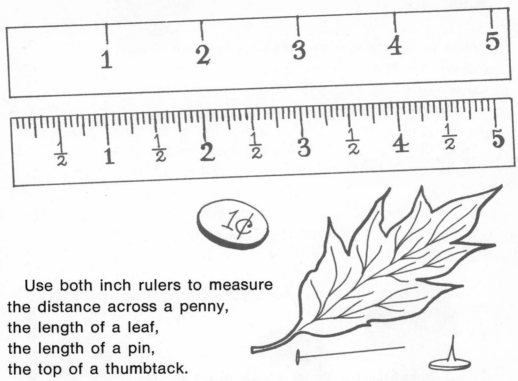

Use both inch rulers to measure
the distance across a penny,
the length of a leaf,
the length of a pin,
the top of a thumbtack.

The ruler marked in inches will give you an approximate measure.

The other ruler will give you a more exact measure.

THINK FOR YOURSELF

Use a magnifying glass and the ruler you just made to check your "exact" measurements. Is there such a thing as an "exact" measurement?

41

GUESSING

How good are you at guessing, or estimating, measurements?

It is not always possible to measure something.

Sometimes you have to guess. You do that by comparing the thing, in your mind, with some unit of measure you know.

Guess how wide you are, compared to a door.

Guess how wide you are, compared to the length of your first finger.

Look around the room. What do you see that you think is 1 inch long? 6 inches long? 1 foot long?

42

How far do you estimate it is from the floor to the ceiling of the room you are in? How far from your house to your school?

When you have a chance, measure to check your guesses. Are you a good estimator?

THINK FOR YOURSELF

What is the smallest thing you can think of?

How small do you think it is?

Could you measure it?

What is the biggest thing you can think of?

How big do you think it is?

Could you think of a way to measure it?

MEASURING IN TWO DIRECTIONS

Suppose you want to paint the wall of a room.
How much paint will you need?
To know that, you have to find out how big the wall is.
Finding out that it is 10 feet long is not enough.
Finding out that it is 8 feet high is not enough.
But if you multiply those two numbers, 8 x 10, you get a measurement called *square* measure or *area* measure.
The area of the wall is 80 square feet. You need enough paint to cover 80 square feet of wall.
Square measure is handy for measuring all kinds of things — the size of a wall or a field or a town or even a whole country.

Could you find square measure without linear measure?

Take some graph paper, or make a grid like this.

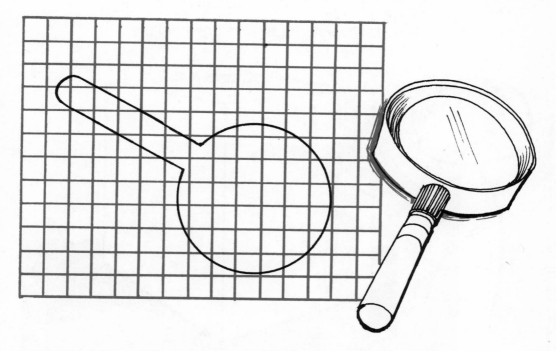

Put any small object on the grid and trace around it.
Count the squares in the tracing.
Is that another way to find square measure?

MEASURING IN THREE DIRECTIONS

You can measure how long a room is and how high it is. But that does not tell you everything about the size of the room.

You can measure how long and how high a box is. But that does not tell you everything about the size of the box.

To really know about the size of the room or the box or any other space shape, you have to measure in three directions: how long, how high, and how wide.

2 feet wide
3 feet high
2 feet long

Then, if you multiply those three numbers together, you get a measurement that tells you something else.

It tells you the *volume* of the shape. Volume means how much space it takes up.

Even if the shape you are measuring is not square all around, as a cube is, the measurement you get is called *cubic* measure. You give the measurement in cubic inches or cubic feet or cubic yards.

$2 \times 3 \times 2 = 12$ cubic feet

WHAT DO YOU THINK?

Could you find cubic measure without knowing linear measure?

TRY IT YOURSELF

What is the volume of a box 3 inches by 3 inches by 3 inches?

Suppose you have a box 1 foot long, 1 foot wide, and 1 foot high. Does the box take up the same amount of space if it is empty,

or made of solid wood,

or full of water?

48

Does the volume of the box change if you pour out the water?

Could you measure the volume of the water in the box?

How could you do that?

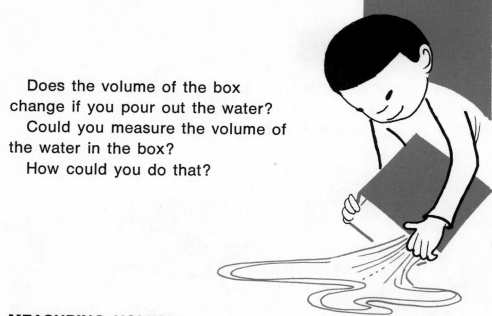

MEASURING VOLUME

Volume is the amount of space anything takes up.

Air takes up space.

Water takes up space.

Ice cream takes up space.

A box takes up space.

If you can measure the volume of a box, you can measure the volume of anything that fills the box, whether it is air, water, or ice cream.

49

When you fill a container, is it always completely full?

Is it really full, even if it is filled to the top? Or does that depend on what you fill it with?

Is the basket full of apples?

Is the pail full of sand?

50

Fill a cup with blueberries. (Or use pebbles or dried beans.)

Is the cup full?
It looks full.

Now pour in some sugar.
What happens to the sugar?
What can you tell from that?
When the sugar is level with the top of the cup, is the cup full now?
Can you think of any way to find out?

Can you measure the volume of something that is not in a container?

How can you measure the volume of water in a puddle?

How can you measure the volume of the blueberries on a bush?

52

How could you get
all the water up
to measure it?

If you use a cup and fill it over and over from the puddle, you can measure how many cups of water are in the puddle.

You can measure the blueberries with a cup too, or with a box. How many times can you fill the box with blueberries from the bush?

Now suppose you tell somebody that you picked a box of blueberries from the bush.

How would he know if you picked

this many   or this many   or this many ?

He wouldn't, unless he knew what *unit of capacity* you used.

There are standard units of capacity in the English system and in the metric system.
In the English system,
1 bushel = 4 pecks,

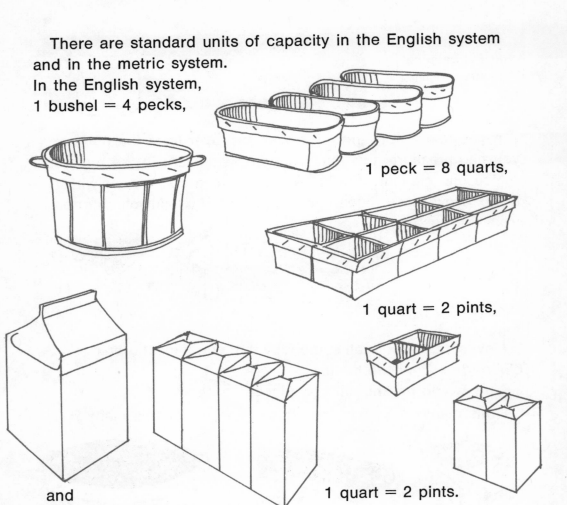

1 peck = 8 quarts,

1 quart = 2 pints,

1 quart = 2 pints.

and
1 gallon = 4 quarts,

In the metric system the standard unit of capacity is the liter (LEE-ter). (Another name for the liter is the cubic decimeter. Can you see why?)

$\frac{1}{10}$ meter

$\frac{1}{10}$ Meter

$\frac{1}{10}$ Meter

Can you guess how other metric units of capacity are related to the liter? Can you guess some of their names?

Can you make up your own units of capacity?
Can you measure with them?

Try
soup bowls,
fishbowls,
eggshells,
saltshakers,
trash baskets.

What other units can you think of?
Would you use different units for measuring small amounts than you use for measuring big amounts?
Now can you put units together to make up your own system for measuring capacity?

Does the unit you use to measure volume change the volume of the stuff you are measuring?

Does the shape of the unit change the volume?

Fill a cup with water.

Pour the water into a pint bottle. (Don't spill any.)

Does the water take up all the space in the bottle?

56

Do you think the volume of the water has changed?

Now pour the water into a quart bottle.

About how much space does it take up in the bottle?

Do you think the volume of the water has changed?

Now pour the water into a square baking tin.

Do you think the volume has changed?

Pour the water into a big soup pot.
Do you think the volume has changed?
Pour the water into a plastic bag.
Do you think the volume has changed?

Pour the water back into the cup to see.

Does the capacity of the container change the volume of the water?

Does the shape of the container change the volume?

WEIGHING IS ANOTHER WAY OF MEASURING

If you look at two objects
and you do not know what they are made of,
you cannot guess from their size how much they weigh.
You cannot even guess which one is heavier.

You could easily carry a pillow bigger than you are. But
you might find it hard just to lift a rock only the size of your
head.

A marshmallow and a lump of lead might be exactly the same size and shape. They could have the same volume. But the lead would weigh much, much more than the marshmallow. That is because there is a lot more stuff in the lump of lead than there is in the marshmallow.

The more stuff something has, the more Earth's gravity pulls on it, so the heavier it is.

When we weigh something, we are really measuring the pull of Earth's gravity on that thing.

Gravity pulls harder on a bowling ball than on a basketball. That is why a bowling ball is heavier.

People learned to measure length, size, area, and capacity before they learned how to measure weight.

WHAT DO YOU THINK?

Do you think that might be because it is easier to see how big something is and how much a container holds?

Can you see how much something weighs, by looking at it?

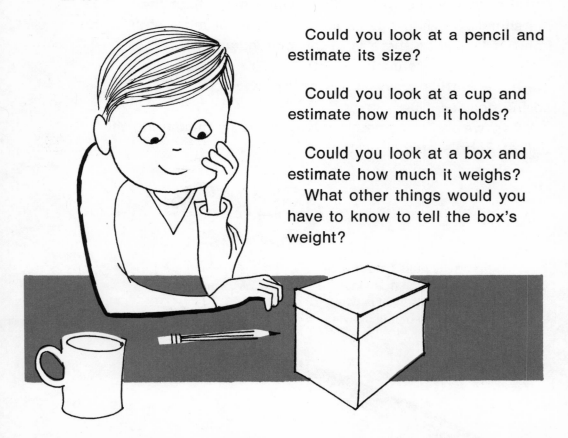

Could you look at a pencil and estimate its size?

Could you look at a cup and estimate how much it holds?

Could you look at a box and estimate how much it weighs?

What other things would you have to know to tell the box's weight?

Take a pencil, an eraser, a small pair of scissors, a marker, a cookie, a small stone, a roll of tape, and some other small objects.

See if you can put them in order, from the lightest to the heaviest, just by looking at them.

Now hold them two at a time, one thing in each hand. Can you feel which is heavier?

Arrange them again, from the lightest to the heaviest. Has the order changed?

Afterward, check your findings on a small postal scale or balance.

Can you invent units for measuring weight, the way you invented units for measuring length and capacity?

Try using seeds, pebbles, paper clips, dried beans, marbles, blocks, cans of soup, beanbags.

THINK FOR YOURSELF

Will it make a difference if the seeds or marbles or cans are not all the same size?

What weighs about the same as 50 seeds?

As 4 marbles?

As 10 cans of soup?

How many cans of soup do you think *you* weigh?

Can you invent a system of weights in which a number of smaller units equals a larger unit?

THINK FOR YOURSELF

Could you measure weight without knowing how to measure length or capacity?

64

DO IT YOURSELF

Make a scale like this, using the small unit of weight you have chosen.

Can you figure out how to mark the scale?

Use heavy cardboard or a piece of cardboard box.

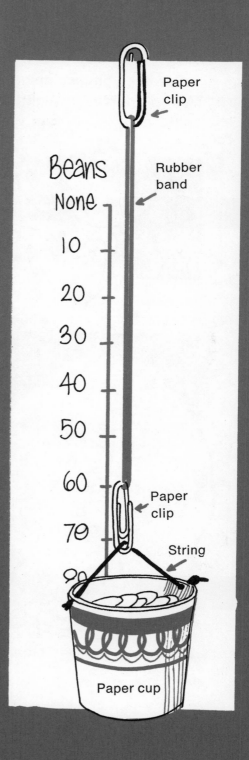

Paper clip

Rubber band

Beans
None
10
20
30
40
50
60
70
90

Paper clip

String

Paper cup

For everyday weighing we use a system called *avoirdupois* (AV-ud-uh-POIZ) weight. These are some of the standard units.

27-11/32 grains = 1 dram

16 drams = 1 ounce

16 ounces = 1 pound

2,000 pounds = 1 ton

In the metric system the gram is the standard unit of weight.

Each smaller unit is 1/10 of the unit before it.

What do you think a decigram is?

What do you think a centigram is?

Each bigger unit is 10 times bigger than the unit before it.

A kilogram equals 1,000 grams.

A kilogram is 2.205 pounds.
If you weigh 75 pounds,
you weigh about 165 kilograms

WHAT DO YOU THINK?

Do you think there is any relation between the metric units of length and weight?

You're right! A standard kilogram is a liter, filled with water.

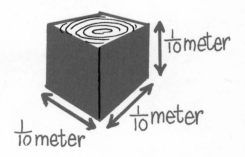

67

HOW MANY WAYS OF MEASURING ARE THERE?

It seems as if there are a lot of ways to measure things.

But if you learn to measure length, capacity, and weight,
and if you can tell time,
you can measure anything.

All the measuring instruments we have, no matter how complicated they seem, measure in one — or more than one — of these ways.

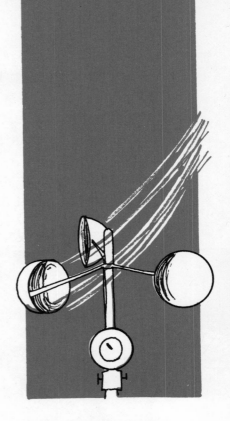

How do you think an anemometer measures the speed of the wind?

A clock measures time. Does it measure distance in any way?

What does a gas gauge measure?

68

What two ways of measuring does a speedometer use?

What does a scale measure?

Radar measures distance by time. Can you guess how?

What way of measuring does a thermometer use for showing the temperature?

What does a water meter measure?

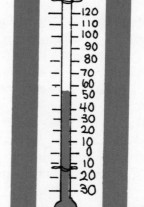

THINK FOR YOURSELF

Why do so many instruments have the word "meter" in their names? What do you think that word means?

Page 22. A mile is 5,280 feet.

Page 26. Yes.

Measure around the ball with a string, then compare the length of the string with a ruler.

Page 27. Yes.

"How far?" means "How long in distance?".

Page 31. 1/2 inch is 1/24 of 1 foot, and 1/72 of 1 yard.

Page 33. 100. "Centi" means 1/100. "Milli" means 1/1000.

Page 35. Measurements in the metric system are easier to work with, because all you have to do is divide or multiply by 10.

Page 41. There is not really an "exact" measurement.

Page 47. No, you cannot find cubic measure without knowing linear measure.

The volume of the box is 27 cubic inches.

Page 48. The box always takes up the same amount of space.

Page 49. Measure the water into a cup.

Page 51. Slowly pour in milk or water. The cup is not full until the liquid drips over.

Page 53. Use a sponge and squeeze the water into the cup.

Page 62. You must know what is in the box and how full the box is.

Page 64. Yes. Choose one size to be a standard unit. You do not need to know length or capacity to measure weight.

Page 65. Mark the scale by putting each number of units in the cup, then marking the place where it hangs on the scale.

Page 68. Yes. The distance the hands travel helps you to tell time.

Wind speed is measured by the number of times the anemometer's cups go around in a certain time.

A gas gauge measures the capacity of the gas tank and how full it is.

Page 69. A speedometer measures time and distance.

A scale measures the pull of gravity on the object being weighed.

Radar measures distance by the time it takes the radar signal to reach the object and reflect to where it came from.

A water meter measures the amount of water that flows through a pipe.

You read the temperature by the distance the colored line rises or falls on the scale.

"Meter" means "measure."

INDEX

Jeanne Bendick is well known as an illustrator and the author of many science books for young people. She is a graduate of New York School of Fine and Applied Arts and first started writing during World War II, when her husband was overseas with the Air Force.

Besides her work in the book field, she and her husband are now designing learning systems using both written materials and films.

She sometimes works on two or three books at a time. "I get a fresher approach if I shift gears," she says.

As her hobbies, Mrs. Bendick lists working, cooking, sailing, and beachcombing.